WILLY THE TEXAS LONGHORN

By Alan C. Elliott

Illustrated by Stephanie Ford

PELICAN PUBLISHING COMPANY

GRETNA 2013

For Mary, John, Angela, Ryan,
William, Melanie, and Scott—A.C.E.
To Sadie, my little cowgirl—S.F.

The word "Pelican" and the depiction of a pelican are
trademarks of Pelican Publishing Company, Inc., and are
registered in the U.S. Patent and Trademark Office.

Library of Congress Cataloging-in-Publication Data

Elliott, Alan C., 1952-
  Willy the Texas longhorn / by Alan C. Elliott ; illustrated by Stephanie Ford.
      pages cm
  Summary: Willy writes a letter to Santa asking to help pull the sleigh, and gets his wish one Christmas Eve when the fog over Texas is pea-soup thick but Willy's horns, painted fluorescent blue, guide their way.
  ISBN 978-1-4556-1870-5 (hardcover : alk. paper) — ISBN 978-1-4556-1871-2 (e-book) [1. Stories in rhyme. 2. Texas longhorn cattle—Fiction. 3. Cattle—Fiction. 4. Santa Claus—Fiction. 5. Christmas—Fiction. 6. Texas—Fiction.] I. Ford, Stephanie (Stephanie H.), illustrator. II. Title.
  PZ8.3.E48Wil 2013
  [E]—dc23

                                        2013014674

Printed in Malaysia
Published by Pelican Publishing Company, Inc.
1000 Burmaster Street, Gretna, Louisiana 70053

Once upon a Christmas Eve,
   down in the Lone Star State,
Something special happened then,
   on that partic'lar date.

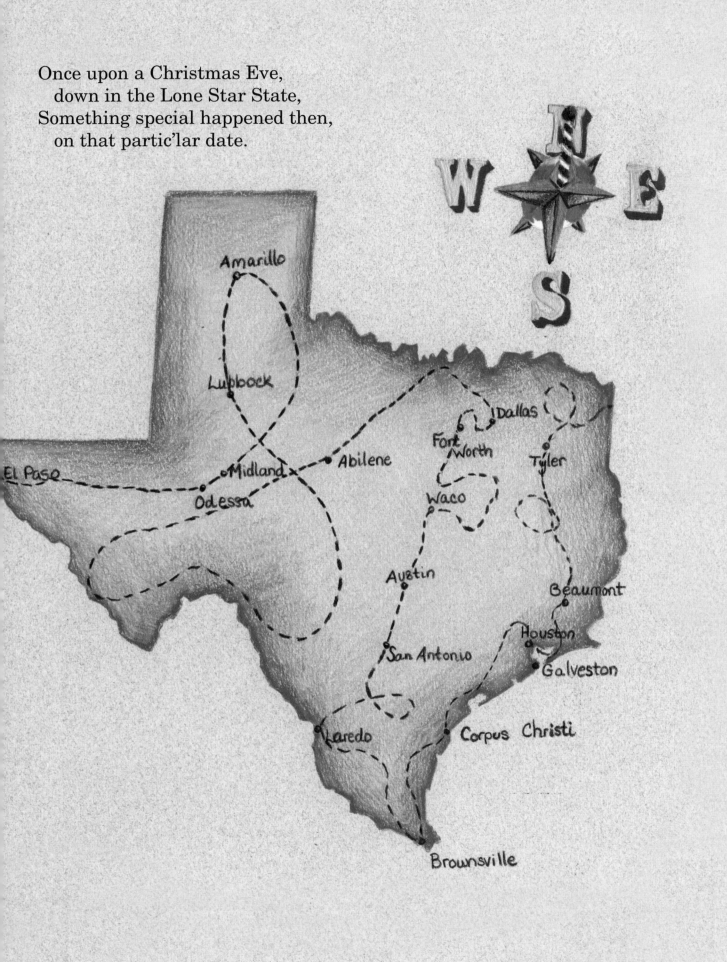

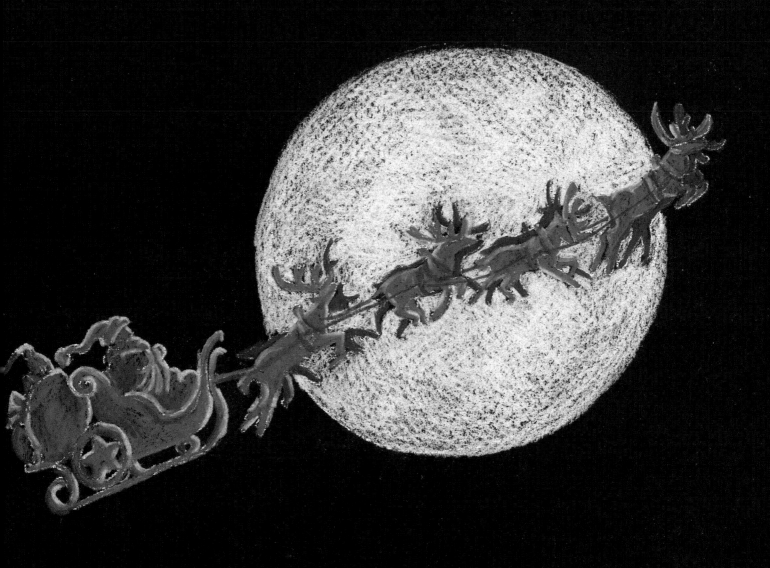

Willy, the Texas Longhorn, no ordinary steer,
Had a kinda crazy dream: to fly like Santa's deer.

His four-hoofed friends said,
   "Willy, no steer will ever fly,
Keep your hooves down on the ground,
   and not up in the sky.
Don't be so highfalutin,
   a cow is just a cow.
Give up your fancy dreamin',
   come down to earth right now."

But Willy kept on thinking that if a deer could soar,
Why then, a clever longhorn could do it even more.
And so he wrote to Santa, "Next time you come this way,
Yessir, I'd be mighty proud, to help you pull your sleigh."

When Texans take a hank'rin to any crazy plan,
There's no telling 'em they can't—cause they
believe they can.
And so one night, when pea-soup fog covered dale
and hill,
And Santa needed help, and fast, Willy said, "I will."

He painted up his long horns a bright,
   fluorescent blue,
And with a puff of Santa dust,
   through the air he flew.
His neon horns showed the way;
   they lit the sky with ease.
That sleigh flew down the Chisholm Trail,
   pretty as you please.

Willy the Texas Longhorn,
   his crazy dream came true,
He flew that sleigh 'cross Texas,
   with horns a'glowing blue,
And kids woke up that morning,
   with happy Christmas smiles
'Cause Willy helped ol' Santa fly 'cross those
   Texas miles.

Plum across the Lone Star State,
    that Christmas sleigh took flight,
Past Caverns of Sonora and through
    the Marfa lights.
From tumbleweeds to tall pine trees,
    they traveled all around,
Through Barton Springs to Sundance Square,
    and into Big D Town.

From Galveston to Corpus, and to the Alamo,

Round the bend of old Big Bend, and on to El Paso.

Through mist and fog and snowflakes, he flew that
     sleigh with style,
From Dalhart, on past Lubbock, and down to Padre Isle.

They flew past San Jacinto,
and swooped by NASA town,

Around Sam Houston's statue, and headed homeward bound.

He pert near set a record,
  that foggy Christmas night,
When blue-horned Willy Longhorn
  helped him make his flight.

And so each Christmas season, come rain,
 or sleet, or snow,
Willy flies the Texas skies,
 with Santa's sleigh in tow,
And there you have the legend,
 of how that longhorn flew,
It seems that Willy's crazy dream
 really did come true.

Willy the Texas Longhorn,
　his crazy dream came true,
He flew that sleigh 'cross Texas,
　with horns a'glowing blue,
And kids woke up that morning,
　with happy Christmas smiles
'Cause Willy helped ol' Santa fly 'cross those
　Texas miles.

Moooo . . . eee Christmas!